THE THREE FISHING BROTHERS GRUFF.

this book is dedicated to my father

THE THREE FISHING BROTHERS GRUFF

By BEN GALBRAITH

Hodder Children's Books

A division of Hachette Children's Books

In three dirty shacks,
in a town called
Poverty Bay,
there lived three
mean,
prickly-faced
fishing brothers.

The youngest brother, Anglo Gruff, was mean and greedy and he owned the smallest boat, a dinghy named Whipper Snapper.

The middle brother, Anvil Gruff, was even meaner and greedier and he owned a medium-sized trawler named Crawler.

Even meaner and greedier was the eldest, Angora Gruff, and he owned a huge fishing vessel called The Cods Wallop.

Every morning the brothers would set out in their boats, returning at dusk with tons of fish.

But one day, the
with only a sm
the next day, th
with nothing.

"It's your fault s
snarled Anvil
"You take far m

"No, it's Anglo's f
Angora. "He ta
before they've gr

"What about you
snarled Anglo to
Crawler leaks o
poisoned the fish

"Well Poverty B
empty," said An
are plenty more

But one day, they came back with only a small catch. And the next day, they came home with nothing.

"It's your fault sea slug," snarled Anvil to Angora. "You take far more than you need."

"No, it's Anglo's fault," hissed Angora. "He takes the little fish before they've grown."

"What about you, fish breath?" snarled Anglo to Anvil. "The Crawler leaks oil. You probably poisoned the fish."

"Well Poverty Bay might be empty," said Angora, "but there are plenty more fish in the sea."

Next Anvil Gruff decided to try his luck.

"Who's that motoring into my bay?"
Minke Whale called.
"Stop or I'll flatten you with my tail!"

"Please don't," pleaded Anvil. "I'm no threat to the sea.
Wait until my older brother Angora Gruff
comes along. His boat is gigantic and he could
catch all the fish in your bay."

Minke Whale thought this over.
"Very well, but don't you dare poison the sea.
Be off with you. I'll wait un—"

The following years were good for
the three brothers Gruff. They became *very* rich
and without **Mink**e to stop them they
fished and fished until...

In the middle of the ocean, with no fishing gear,
the three brothers played cards to pass the time.

HAPPY FAMILIES was no fun.
SNAP was boring.
And they cheated at FISH.

"Hey! Did anyone see that?" said Anglo.
"I think I just saw a whale…"

Minke rammed The Cods Wallop so hard that all three brothers ended up in the sea.

In one gulp, she swallowed Anglo, the youngest brother.

With a swipe of her tail, Anvil, the middle brother, went to the bottom of the ocean.

PLEASE FOLLOW FISHING RULES TO GIVE US A CHANCE TO GROW BIGGER.

As for Angora, the oldest brother... let's just say he was fish food.

Once the three brothers Gruff had gone,
ever so slowly, the sea life came back
to the bays. The people of both towns had
learnt a lot. No more did they dirty
the water with oil or rubbish and
they were careful never to be greedy.
They only took enough fish to feed
themselves, and they left the smaller fish
to grow big for another day.

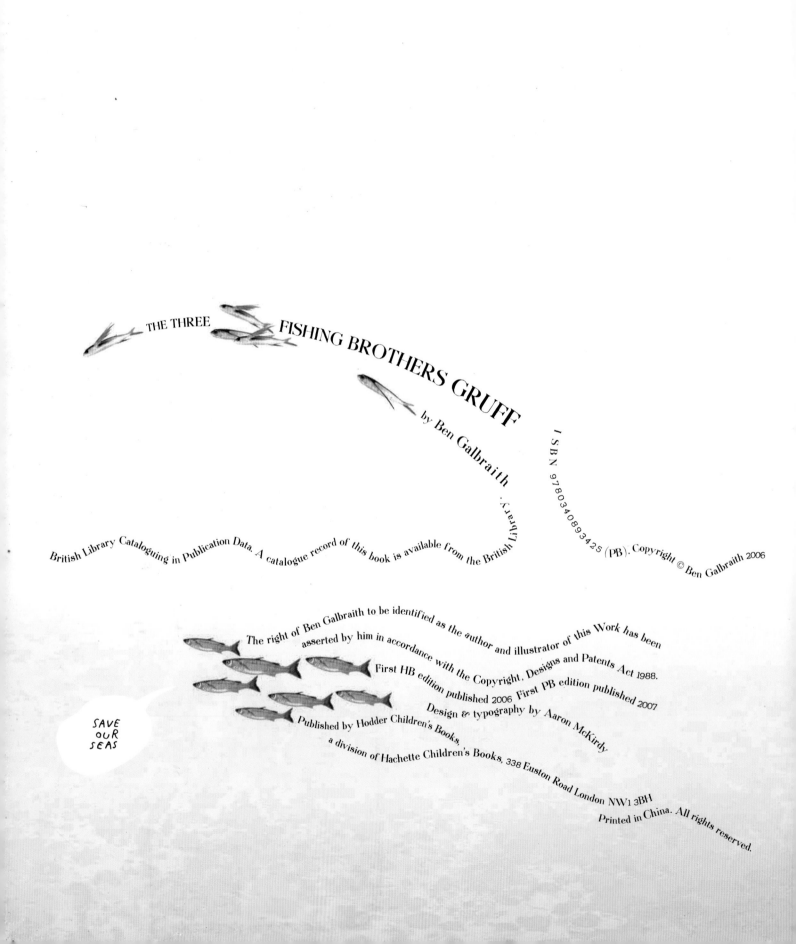

THE THREE FISHING BROTHERS GRUFF

by Ben Galbraith

I S B N 9780340893425 (PB). Copyright © Ben Galbraith 2006

British Library Cataloguing in Publication Data. A catalogue record of this book is available from the British Library.

The right of Ben Galbraith to be identified as the author and illustrator of this Work has been asserted by him in accordance with the Copyright, Designs and Patents Act 1988. First HB edition published 2006 First PB edition published 2007 Design & typography by Aaron McKirdy. Published by Hodder Children's Books, a division of Hachette Children's Books, 338 Euston Road London NW1 3BH

SAVE OUR SEAS